Œdipus

Voltaire

Translation by William F. Fleming

Start Publishing PD is a registered trademark of Start Publishing PD LLC
Manufactured in the United States of America

Cover art: Shutterstock/Taisiya Kozorez

Cover design: Jennifer Do

10 9 8 7 6 5 4 3 2 1

ISBN 979-8-8809-0384-9

Contents

Dramatis Personæ

Œdipus, King of Thebes.
Jocaste, Queen of Thebes.
Philoctetes, Prince of Eubæa.
High Priest.
Araspes, Confidant of Œdipus.
Ægina, Confidante of Jocaste.
Dimas, Friend of Philoctetes.
Phorbas, an old Man of Thebes.
Icarus, an old Man of Corinth.
Chorus of Thebans.

SCENE Thebes.

Œdipus was written when M. de Voltaire was but nineteen years of age. It was played for the first time in 1718, and ran five-and-forty nights. Du Frêsne, a celebrated actor, and of the same age with the author, played the part of Œdipus; and Madame Desmarêts, a famous actress, did Jocaste, and soon after quitted the stage. In this edition, the part of Philoctetes is restored, and stands exactly as it was in the first representation.

ACT I.

Philoctetes, Dimas.

Dimas: Is it my friend, my Philoctetes? Whence And wherefore comest thou to distempered Thebes In search of death, to brave the wrath of heaven? For, know, the gods on this devoted land Wreak their full vengeance: mortals dare not tread The guilty soil, to death and horror long Consigned, and from the living world cut off: Away, begone!

Philoctetes: It suits a wretch like me: Leave me, my friend, to my unhappy fate; And only tell me, if the wrath divine Hath, in its rapid progress, spared the queen.

Dimas: Jocaste lives; but round her throne still spreads The dire contagion; every fatal moment Deprives her of some faithful subject: death Steals closer by degrees, and seems to threat Her sacred life. But heaven, we trust, will soon Withdraw its vengeful arm: such scenes of blood Will sure appease its rage.

Philoctetes: What horrid crime Could bring down so severe a punishment?

Dimas: Since the king's death—

Philoctetes: The king! ha! Laius—

Dimas: Died Some four years since.

Philoctetes: Ha! Laius dead! indeed! What sweet seducing hope awakes my soul? Jocaste! will the gods at length be kind? May Philoctetes still be thine? But say, Dimas, how fell the king?

Dimas: 'Tis four years since For the last time towards Bœotia, led By fate, you came; scarce had you bent your way To Asia, e'er the unhappy Laius fell By some base hand.

Philoctetes: Assassinated, sayest thou?

Dimas: This was the cause, the source of all our ills, The ruin of this wretched country: shocked At the sad stroke, we wept the general loss, When lo! the minister of wrath divine, (Fatal to innocence, and favoring long Unpunished guilt) a dreadful monster came, (O Philoctetes, would thou hadst been here!) And ravaged all our borders, horrid form! Made for destruction by avenging heaven, With human voice, an eagle, woman, lion, Unnatural mixture! rage with cunning joined United to destroy us: naught remained To save but this alone; in phrase obscure The monster had proposed to affrighted Thebes A strange enigma, which who could unfold Should save his country; if he failed, must die. Reluctant we obeyed the hard decree. Instant the general voice aloud proclaimed The kingdom his reward, who, by the gods Inspired, should first unveil the mystery. The aged and the wise, by hope misled, With fruitless science braved the monster's rage; Vain knowledge all! all tried and trying fell, Till Œdipus, the heir to Corinth's throne, Endowed with wisdom far above his years, Fearless, and led by fortune, came, beheld, Unfolded all, and took the great reward; Lives still, and reigns o'er Thebes; but reigns, alas! O'er dying subjects, and a desert land. Vainly we hoped to see the wayward fates Chained to his throne, and yielding to the hand Of Œdipus, our great deliverer. A little time the gods propitious smiled, And blessed us with a gleam of transient peace; But barrenness and famine soon destroyed Our airy hopes: ills heaped on ills succeed, A dreadful plague unpeoples half the realms Of sickly Thebes, snatching the poor remains Just escaped from famine and the grave: high heaven Hath thus ordained, and such our hapless fate. But say, illustrious hero, whom the gods Have long approved, say, wherefore hast thou left The paths of glory, and the smiles of fortune, To seek the regions of affliction here?

Philoctetes: I come to join my sorrows and my tears, For know the world with me hath lost its best And noblest friend: ne'er shall these eyes behold The offspring of the gods, like them unconquered, Earth's best support, the guardian deity Of innocence oppressed: I mourn a friend, The world a father.

Dimas: Is Alcides dead?

Philoctetes: These hands performed the melancholy office, Laid on his funeral pile the first of men; The all-conquering arrows, those dear dreadful gifts The son of Jove bequeathed me, have I brought, With his cold ashes, here, where I will raise A tomb and altars to my valued friend. O! had he lived! had but indulgent heaven, In pity to mankind, prolonged his days, Far from Jocaste I had still remained; And, though I might have cherished still my vain And hopeless passion, had not wandered here, Or left Alcides for a woman's love.

Dimas: Oft have I pitied thy unhappy flame, Caught in thy earliest youth, increasing still And growing with thy growth: Jocaste, forced By a hard father to a hateful bed, Unwillingly partook the throne of Laius. Alas! what tears those fatal nuptials cost, What sorrows have they brought on wretched Thebes! How have I oft admired thy noble soul, Worthy of empire! conqueror o'er thyself: There first the hero shone, repressed his passion, And the first tyrant he subdued was love.

Philoctetes: There we must fly to conquer; I confess it: Long time I strove, I felt my weakness long; At length resolved to shun the fatal place, I took a last farewell of my Jocaste. The world then trembled at Alcides' name, And on his valor did suspend their fate; I joined the god-like man, partook his toils, Marched by his side, and twined his laurel wreath Round my own brows: then my enlightened soul Against the passions armed, and rose superior. A great man's friendship is the gift of heaven. In him I read my duty and my fate; I bound myself to virtue and to him: My valor strengthened, and my heart improved, Not hardened, I became like my Alcides. What had I been without him! a king's son, A common prince, the slave of every passion, Which Hercules hath taught me to subdue.

Dimas: Now then unmoved thou canst behold Jocaste, And her new husband.

Philoctetes: Ha! another husband! Saidst thou, another?

Dimas: Œdipus hath joined To hers his future fate

Philoctetes: He is too happy; But he is worthy: he who saved a kingdom Alone can merit her, and heaven is just.

Dimas: He comes, and with him his assembled people; Lo! the high-priest attends: this way they bend, To deprecate the wrath of angry heaven.

Philoctetes: It melts my soul; I weep for their misfortunes. O Hercules, from thy eternal seat Look down on thy afflicted country! hear Thy fellow citizens! O hear thy friend, Who joins his prayers, and be their guardian god!

SCENE II.

High Priest, Chorus.

First Person of the Chorus: Ye blasting powers, who waste this wretched empire, And breathe contagion, death, and horrors round us, O quicken your slow wrath, be kind at last, And urge our lingering fate.

Second Person of the Chorus: Strike, strike, ye gods, Your victims are prepared; ye mountains, fall! Crush us, ye heavens! O death, deliver us, And we shall thank you for the boon.

High Priest: No more: Cease your loud plaints, the wretch's poor resource; Yield to the power supreme, who means to try His people by affliction; with a word He can destroy, and with a word can save: He knows that death is here; the cries of Thebes Have reached his throne. Behold! the king approaches, And heaven by me declares its will divine; The fates will soon to Œdipus unveil Their mysteries all, and happier days succeed.

SCENE III.

Œdipus, Jocaste, High Priest, Ægina, Dimas, Araspes, Chorus.

Œdipus: O ye, who to this hallowed temple bring The mournful offering of your tears: O what, What shall I say to my afflicted people? Would I could turn the wrath of angry heaven Against myself, and quench the deadly flame? But O! in universal ills like these, Kings are but men, and only can partake The common danger. Say, thou minister Of the just gods, say, do they still refuse To hear the voice of misery; still relentless Will they behold us perish, are they deaf And silent still?

High Priest: King, people, listen all: This night did I behold the flame of heaven Descending on our altars; to my eyes The ghastly shade of Laius then appeared, Indignant frowned upon me, and thus spoke In fearful accents, terrible to hear: "The death of Laius is still unrevenged, The murderer lives in Thebes, and doth infect The wholesome air with his malignant breath; He must be known, he must be punished, And on his fate depends the people's safety."

Œdipus: Justly ye suffer, Thebans, for this crime; Laius was once your loved and honored king, And your neglect hath from his manes drawn This vengeance on you. Such is oft the fate Of the best sovereigns; whilst they live, respect Waits on their laws, their justice is admired, And they like gods are served, like gods adored; But after death they sink into oblivion. No longer then your flattering incense burns: The servile mind of wretched man still bends To interest; and when virtue is departed, 'Tis soon forgotten: therefore doth the blood Of murdered Laius now cry out against you, And sues for vengeance to offended heaven. To sprinkle on his tomb the murderer's blood Will better far than slaughtered hecatombs Appease his spirit: be it all our care To seek the guilty wretch. Can none remember Aught touching this sad deed? Amidst your signs And wonders, could no footsteps e'er be traced Of this unpunished crime? They always told me It was a Theban, who against his prince Uplifted his rebellious hand. For me [To Jocaste.] Who from thy hands received the crown, two years After the death of Laius did I mount The throne of Thebes, and never since that hour Would I recall the subject of thy tears, But in respectful silence waited still; Still have thy dangers busied all my soul, Nor left me time to think on aught but thee.

Jocaste: When fate, which had reserved me for thy arms, Deprived me of my late unhappy lord, Who, journeying o'er his kingdom's frontiers, fell By base assassins, Phorbas then alone Attended him, his loved and valued friend; To whom the king, relying on his wisdom, Entrusted half his power: he brought to Thebes The mangled corpse: himself half dead with wounds, And bathed in blood, fell at Jocaste's feet; "Villains unknown," he cried, "have slain the king; These eyes beheld it: I was dying too, But heaven hath restored me to prolong A wretched life." He said no more. My soul Distracted saw the melancholy truth Was still concealed; and therefore heaven perhaps Concealed the murderer too; perhaps accomplished Its own eternal will, and made us guilty, That it might punish. Soon the sphinx appeared, And laid our country waste: then hapless Thebes, Attentive to her safety, could not think On Laius' fate, whilst trembling for her own.

Œdipus: Where is that faithful Phorbas? lives he still?

Jocaste: Alas! his zeal and service ill repaid, Too powerful to be loved, the jealous state His secret foe, nobles and people joined To punish him for past felicity. The multitude accused him, even demanded Of me his death: sore pressed on every side, I knew not how to pardon or condemn, But to a neighboring castle I conveyed him, And hid the guiltless victim from their rage. There four long winters hath the poor old man, To future favorites a sad example, Without a murmur or complaint remained, And hopes from innocence alone release.

Œdipus: It is enough, Jocaste. Fly, begone, [To his servants.] Open the prison, bring him hither straight, We will examine him before you all; Laius and Thebes shall be avenged together: Yes, we will hear and judge, will sound the depth Of this strange mystery. Ye gods of Thebes, Who hear our prayers, and know the murderer, now Reveal, and punish; and thou, Sun, withhold From his dark eyes thy blessed light! proscribed, Abandoned, let him wander o'er the earth A wretched miscreant, by his sons abhorred, And to his mother horrible! deprived Of burial, let his body be the prey Of hungry vultures!

High Priest: In these execrations We all unite.

Œdipus: Gods! let the guilty suffer, And they alone! or if the high decrees Of your eternal justice leave to me His punishment, at least indulgent grant, Where you command, the power to obey; If you pursue the guilty, O complete The glorious work, and make the victim known! [To the people.] Return, my people, to the temple; there Once more entreat the gods: perhaps your prayers May from their heavenly mansions draw them down To dwell among us: if they loved the king, They will avenge his death, and kind to him Who errs unknowing, will direct this arm For justice raised, and teach me where to strike.

ACT II.

SCENE I.

Jocaste, Ægina, Araspes, Chorus.

Araspe: Believe me, 'tis too true, my royal mistress, Your dying people, with one common voice, Accuse the hapless Philoctetes: fate Hath sent him back to save this wretched kingdom.

Jocaste: What do I hear, ye powers?

Ægina: 'Tis wonderful.

Jocaste: Who? Philoctetes?

Araspe: Yes, it must be he: To whom can we impute it but to him? When last at Thebes, he seemed to meditate A deed like this; for much he hated Laius: From Œdipus his traitorous purpose scarce Could he conceal; for soon unwary youth Betrays itself: soon through the thin disguise Of ill dissembled loyalty, we saw The rancor of his heart. I know not what Provoked him, but too warm and open, ever The slave of passion, he would kindle oft At the king's name, and often pour forth threats Of vengeance: for some time he left the kingdom, But fate soon brought the restless wanderer back; And at that fatal time, which heaven distinguished By the detested shocking parricide, He was at Thebes: e'er since that dreadful hour, Suspicion justly falls on Philoctetes: But the high name which he had gained in war, His boasted title of earth's great avenger, And his heroic deeds, have stopped the tongue Of clamor, and suspended yet the stroke Of our resentment. Now the time is come When Thebes shall think no more of vain respect; His glory and his conquests plead no more; The hearts of an oppressed people groan; The gods require his blood, and must be heard.

Chorus: O queen! have pity on a wretched people, Who love and honor thee, revere the gods, And follow their example; yield up to us Their victim, and present our vows to heaven; For heaven will hear them, if they come from thee.

Jocaste: O! if my life can mitigate its wrath, I give it freely; take the sacrifice; Accept my blood; but O! demand no more. Thebans, be gone.

SCENE II.

Jocaste, Ægina.

Ægina: How I lament thy fate!

Jocaste: Alas! I envy those whom death has freed From all their cares: but what remains for me, What pain and torment to a virtuous heart!

Ægina: 'Tis terrible indeed: the clamorous people, Warmed with false zeal, will cry aloud for vengeance, And soon demand their victim. I forbear To accuse him; but if he at last should prove The murderer of thy unhappy lord, How it must shock thy soul!

Jocaste: Impossible! Such guilt and baseness never dwelt in him. O my Ægina! since our bonds of love Were disunited, naught has pierced my heart Like this suspicion: this alone was wanting To make Jocaste most completely wretched: But I'll not bear to hear him thus accused; I loved him, and he must be innocent.

Ægina: That constant love—

Jocaste: Nay, think not that my heart Still nourishes a guilty passion for him; I conquered that long since; yet, dear Ægina, Howe'er the soul may act which virtue guides, Its secret motions, nature's children, still Must force their way: they will not be subdued, But in the folds and windings of the heart, Lurk still, and rush upon us; hid in fires We thought extinguished, from their ashes rise: In the hard conflict, rigid virtue may Resist the passions, but can ne'er destroy them.

Ægina: How just, and yet how noble is thy grief! Such sentiments!—

Jocaste: Jocaste is most wretched; Thou knowest my miseries, and thou knowest my heart, Ægina: twice hath Hymen lit his torch For me, and twice hath changed my slavery, For such it was; the only man I loved, Torn from my arms. Forgive me, ye just gods, The sad remembrance of a conquered passion. Ægina, thou wert witness of our loves, Those ties, alas! dissolved as soon as made: Then Œdipus, my sovereign, sought and gained me, Spite of myself. I took the diadem, Begirt with sorrows. To forget the past Became my duty then; and I obeyed. Thou knowest I stifled every tender thought Of my first love, disguised an aching heart, Drank up my tears, and even from myself Strove to conceal my griefs.

Ægina: How could you venture The dangerous trial of a second marriage?

Jocaste: Alas!

Ægina: Will you forgive me? shall I speak?

Jocaste: Thou mayest.

Ægina: The king, the conqueror subdued thee: You gave your hand as a reward to him Who saved your country.

Jocaste: Gracious gods!

Ægina: Was he Happier than Laius? Was your Philoctetes Forgotten then, or did they share your heart?

Jocaste: Thebes, by a cruel monster then laid waste, Had promised its deliverer my hand; The conqueror of the sphinx was worthy of me.

Ægina: You loved him then?

Jocaste: I felt some tenderness For Œdipus; but O! 'twas far from love: 'Twas not, Ægina, that tumultuous passion, The impetuous offspring of my ravished senses, Not the fierce flame that burned for Philoctetes; Who, by his fatal charms, subdued my reason, And poured love's sweetest poison o'er my heart: Friendship sincere was all I could bestow On Œdipus, for much I prized his virtue; And pleased, beheld him mount the throne of Thebes Which he had saved; but, whilst I followed him, Even at the altar, my affrighted soul, Wherefore I knew not, was most strangely moved, And I retired with horror to his arms. To this a dreadful omen did succeed: Methought, Ægina, in the dead of night, I saw the gulf of hell yawn wide before me; When lo! the spirit of my murdered lord, Bloody and pale, with threatening aspect stood, And pointed to my son; that son, Ægina, Which I to Laius bore, and to the gods Offered, a cruel pious sacrifice. They beckoned me to follow them, and seemed To drag me with them to the horrid gloom Of Tartarus: my troubled soul long kept The sad idea, and must keep it ever. Now Philoctetes doubles every woe.

Ægina: I heard a noise that way, and, see he comes.

Jocaste: 'Tis he; I tremble: but I will avoid him.

SCENE III.

Jocaste, Philoctetes.

Philoctetes: Do not avoid me, do not fly, Jocaste. From Philoctetes; turn, and look upon me: O speak to me, nor fear my jealous tears Should interrupt the new-born happiness Of thy late nuptials: think not that I came To cast reproaches on thee, or with sighs To win thy lost affection; vulgar arts, Unworthy of us both! the heart, Jocaste, That burned for thee, and if I may recall Thy plighted faith, was once not hateful to thee, Has learned, from thy example, not to feel Weakness like that.

Jocaste: I must approve thy conduct, And 'tis but fit I vindicate my own: I loved thee, Philoctetes; but my fate Tore me from thee, and gave me to another. Thou knowest what woes the horrid sphinx, by heaven Appointed to afflict us, brought on Thebes: Too well thou knowest that Œdipus—

Philoctetes: Is thine; I know it, and is worthy of the blessing: Young as he was, his wisdom saved thy country; His virtues, his fair deeds, and what still more Exalted him, Jocaste's love, have ranked Thy Œdipus among the first of men. Wherefore did cruel fortune, still resolved To punish Philoctetes, drive me hence, To seek vain trophies in a distant land? O! if the conqueror of the sphinx was doomed To conquer thee, why was not I at Thebes? I'd not have labored in the fruitless search Of idle mysteries, wrapped in words of darkness; This arm, to conquest long beneath thy smiles Accustomed, should have drawn the vengeful sword, And laid the howling monster at thy feet. But O! a happier arm has wrested from me That noblest triumph, and deserved Jocaste.

Jocaste: Alas! thou knowest not yet what ills await thee.

Philoctetes: Thee and Alcides I have lost already: Is there aught more to fear?

Jocaste: Thou dwellest at Thebes; The detestation of avenging gods; The baneful pestilence stalks forth amongst us; The blood of Laius cries aloud, and heaven Pursues us still: the murderer must bleed; He has been sought for; some have dared to say That he is found, and call him Philoctetes.

Philoctetes: Astonishment! the base suspicion shocks My soul, and bids my tongue be silent ever On the opprobrious theme: accused of murder! Murdering thy husband! thou canst never believe it.

Jocaste: O! never! 'twere injurious to thy honor To combat such imposture, or refute The vile aspersion; no, thou knowest my heart, Thou hadst my love, and couldst not do a deed Unworthy of it. Let them perish all, These worthless Thebans, who deserve their fate For thus suspecting thee: but, hence! begone! Our vows are fruitless: heaven reserves for thee Superior blessings. Thou wert born to serve The gods, whose wisdom would not bury here Virtues like thine, or suffer love to rule A heart designed for universal sway, And courage fit to save and bless mankind. Ill would it suit the follower of Alcides To lose his moments in the fond concerns, The little cares of love. Thy hours are due To the unhappy and the injured: they Will all thy time and all thy virtue claim. Already tyrants throng on every side; Alcides dead, new monsters rise; go, thou, And give the world another Hercules. Œdipus comes; permit me to retire; Not that I fear the weakness of my heart, But as Jocaste loved thee once, and he Is now my husband, I should blush before you.

SCENE IV.

Œdipus, Philoctetes, Araspes.

Œdipus: Sayst thou, Araspes, is he here, the prince, The noble Philoctetes?

Philoctetes: Yes; 'tis he; Led by blind fortune to this hapless clime, Where angry heaven hath made me suffer wrongs I am not used to bear. I know the crimes Laid to my charge; but think not that I mean To justify myself: too well I know thee To think that Œdipus would ever stoop To such low mean suspicions: no! thy fame Is mixed with mine; in the same steps of honor We trod together. Theseus, Hercules, And Philoctetes, pointed out to thee The paths of glory; do not then disgrace Their names, and taint thy own, by calumny, But keep their bright examples still before thee.

Œdipus: All that I wish is but to save my country, And if I can be useful to mankind, This is the ambition I would satisfy, And this the lesson which those heroes taught, Whom thou hast followed, and whom I admire. I meant not to accuse thee: had I chose The people's victim, it had been myself. I think it but the duty of a king To perish for his country: 'tis an honor Too great for common men. Then had I saved Once more my Thebans, yielded up my life, And sheltered thine: but 'twas not in my power. The blood of guilt must flow, thou standest accused. Defend thyself: if thou art innocent, None shall rejoice so much as Œdipus; Nor as a criminal shall then receive thee, But as my noble friend, as Philoctetes.

Philoctetes: I thought myself, indeed, above suspicion: From many a base assassin has this arm, While Jove's dread thunder slept, relieved mankind Whom we chastise, we seldom imitate.

Œdipus: I do not think thou wouldst disgrace thy name, And thy fair martial deeds, by such a crime. If Laius fell by thee, he fell with honor, I doubt it not, for I must do thee justice.

Philoctetes: If I had slain him, I had only gained One added triumph. Kings, indeed, are gods To their own subjects, but to Hercules, Or me, they were no more than common men. I have avenged the wrongs of mighty princes; And, therefore, little, thou mayest think, should fear To attack the bravest.

Œdipus: Heroes, like thyself, Are equal even to kings, I know they are: But still remember, prince, whoe'er slew Laius, His head must answer for the woes of Thebes; And thou—

Philoctetes: I slew him not; let that suffice. If I had done the deed, I would have owned, Nay boasted of it. Hear me, Œdipus, Though vulgar souls, by vulgar methods, deign To vindicate their injured honor; kings And heroes, when they speak, expect, no doubt, To be believed: perhaps thou dost suspect I murdered Laius. It becomes not thee, Of all men, to accuse me: to thy hand

Devolved his sceptre and his queen. Who reaped The fruits of Laius's death, but Œdipus? Who took the spoils? Who filled his throne? Not I. That object never tempted Philoctetes: Alcides never would accept a crown: We knew no master, and desired no subjects: I have made kings, but never wished to be one. But 'tis beneath me to refute the falsehood, For innocence is lessened by defence.

Œdipus: Thy pride offends me, whilst thy virtue charms. If thou art guiltless, thou hast naught to fear From justice and the laws; thy innocence Will shine with double splendor: dwell with us, And wait the event.

Philoctetes: My honor is concerned, And therefore I shall stay; nor hence depart Till I have ample vengeance for the wrongs Thy base suspicions cast on Philoctetes.

SCENE V.

Œdipus, Araspes.

Œdipus: Araspes, I can never think him guilty: A heart like his, intrepid, brave, and fearless, Could never stoop to mean disguise; nor thoughts So noble e'er inspire the timid breast Of falsehood: no! such baseness is far from him: I even blushed to accuse him, and condemned My own injustice: hard and cruel fate Of royalty! alas! kings cannot read The hearts of men, and oft on innocence, Spite of ourselves unjust, inflict the pains Due to the guilty. How this Phorbas lingers! In him alone are all my hopes: the gods Refuse to hear or answer to our vows; Their silence shows how much they are offended.

Araspe: Rely then on thyself: the gods, whose aid This priest hath promised, do not always dwell Within their temples; tripods, caves, and cells, The brazen mouths that pour forth oracles, Which men had framed, by men may be inspired; We must not rest our faith on priests alone; Even in the sanctuary traitors oft May lurk unseen, exert their pious arts To enslave mankind, and bid the destinies Speak or be silent just as they command them. Search then, and find the truth, examine all; Phorbas, and Philoctetes, and Jocaste. Trust to yourself; let our own eyes determine; Be they our tripods, oracles, and gods.

Œdipus: Within the temple, thinkest thou, perfidy Like this can dwell: but if just heaven at last Should fix our fate, and Œdipus be called To execute its will, he will receive The precious trust, the safety of his country, Nor act unworthy of it. To the gods Once more I go, and with incessant prayer Will try to soothe their anger: thou, meantime, If thou wouldst wish to serve me, hasten onward The lingering Phorbas; in our hapless state, I must enquire the truth of gods and men.

ACT III.

SCENE I.

Jocaste, Ægina.

Jocaste: Yes, my Ægina, I expect him here; 'Tis the last time these eyes shall e'er behold The wretched Philoctetes.

Ægina: Thou hast heard, My royal mistress, to what desperate height The clamorous people carry their resentment; Our dying Thebans from his punishment Expect their safety. Old men, women, children, United by misfortunes, breathe forth vengeance; Pronounce him guilty, and cry out that heaven Demands his blood: canst thou resist the torrent, Defend, or save him?

Jocaste: Yes: I will defend him; Even though Thebes should lift the murderous hand Against her queen, beneath her smoking walls To crush Jocaste, ne'er would I betray Such injured innocence; but still I fear The tongue of slander: well thou knowest my heart Once sighed for Philoctetes; now, Ægina, Will they not say I sacrifice to him My fame, my gods, my country, and my husband? Will they not say Jocaste loves him still?

Ægina: Calm thy vain fears; thy passion had no witness But me, and never—

Jocaste: Thinkest thou that a princess Can e'er conceal her hatred or her love? O no! on every side the eager eyes Of courtiers look upon us: through the veil Of feigned respect, with subtle treachery They search our hearts, and trace out every weakness. Naught can escape their sharp malignant sight; A little word, a sigh, or glance betrays us; Our very silence shall be made to speak Our thoughts; and when their busy artifice, Spite of ourselves, hath drawn the secret from us, Then their loud censures cast invidious light O'er all our actions, and the instructed world Is quickly taught to echo every weakness.

Ægina: But what hast thou to fear from calumny? What piercing eye can wound Jocaste's fame? Who knows thy love, will know thy conquest o'er it; Will know thy virtue still supported thee.

Jocaste: It is that virtue which distresses me; I look, perhaps, with too severe an eye On my own weakness, and accuse myself Unjustly; but the image still remains Of Philoctetes, engraved within my heart Too deep for time or virtue to efface it; And much I doubt, if when I strive to save him. I act not less from justice than from love: My pity hath too much of tenderness; I tremble oft, and oft reproach myself For my fond care; I could be more his friend, If he had been less dear to me.

Ægina: But say, Is it your will that he depart?

Jocaste: It is: And O! if he would listen to Jocaste, Never return, never behold me more; Fly from this fatal, this distressful scene, And save my life and fame. But what detains him? Why hastes he not? Ægina, fly—

SCENE II.

Philoctetes, Ægina, Jocaste.

Jocaste: He's here. O prince, my soul is on the rack; I blush To see the man whom duty bids me shun, Which says I should forget and not betray thee. Doubtless thou knowest the dreadful fate that hangs O'er thy devoted head.

Philoctetes: The clamorous people Demand my life; but they have suffered much, And therefore, though unjust, I pity them.

Jocaste: Yield not thyself a victim to their rage: Away, begone; as yet thou art thyself The master of thy fate; but this perhaps Is the last minute that can give me power To save thee: far, O fly far from Jocaste; And, in return for added life, I beg thee But to forget 'twas I who thus preserved it.

Philoctetes: I could have wished, Jocaste, thou hadst shown More strength of mind, and less compassion for me; Preferred with me my honor to my life, And rather bade me die than meanly quit My station here: I yet am innocent, But in obeying thee I should be guilty. Of all the blessings heaven bestowed upon me, My honor and my fame alone remain Untouched. O! do not rob me of a treasure So precious to me; do not make me thus Unworthy of Jocaste. I have lived, Lived to fulfil the fate allotted to me; Have passed my sacred word to

Œdipus, And whatsoever suspicions he may cherish, I am a stranger to the breach of honor.

Jocaste: O Philoctetes, let me here entreat thee, By the just gods, by that ill-fated passion, Which once inspired thy breast, if aught remains Of tender friendship, if thou still rememberest How much my happiness on thine depended, Deign to prolong a glorious life, and days That should have been united with Jocaste.

Philoctetes: To thee devoted I would have them still In equal tenor flow, and worthy of thee; I've lived far from thee, and shall die content, If thy regard attends me to the tomb Who knows but heaven may yet refuse to see This bloody sacrifice; perhaps, in mercy It guided me to Thebes to save Jocaste; Shortened my days, perhaps, to lengthen thine. Happy event! the blood of innocence May be accepted; mine is not unworthy.

SCENE III.

Œdipus, Jocaste, Philoctetes, Ægina, Araspes, with Attendants.

Œdipus: Fear not the clamors of an idle crowd, That rage tumultuous, and demand thy death: Know, Philoctetes, I have calmed their rage And will myself, if needful, be thy guard. I judge not with the hasty multitude, But wish to see thy innocence appear: My doubtful mind, uncertain where to fix, Nor dares or to condemn, or to acquit thee: Heaven can alone determine all, which hears My ardent prayer; at length it seems appeased, And by its priest shall soon point out the victim. The gods shall soon decide 'twixt Thebes and thee.

Philoctetes: Great is thy love of truth, O king, but know Justice extreme is height of injury; We must not always hearken to the voice Of rigor: honor is the first of laws, Let us observe it. But thou seest me sunk Beneath myself, answering the slandrous tongues Of base defamers, whom I should despise. O let not Œdipus unite with such To ruin my fair fame! it is enough That I deny it; 'tis enough to call My life before thee. Let Alcides come, And bring with him the monsters I destroyed, The tyrants I subdued; let these stand forth My witnesses, and let my enemies confute them. But ask your priest whether his gods condemn me; I'll wait their sentence; not because I fear it, But to preserve thy persecuted people.

SCENE IV.

Œdipus, Jocaste, High Priest, Araspes, Philoctetes, Ægina, Attendants, Chorus.

Œdipus: Will heaven at last indulgent to our prayers Withdraw its vengeance? By what murderous hand Was it offended?

Philoctetes: Speak, whose blood must flow For expiation?

High Priest: Fatal gift of heaven! Unhappy knowledge! to what dangers oft Dost thou betray the heart of curious man! O would that fate, thus open to my view, Had o'er its secrets drawn the eternal veil To hide them from my sight!

Philoctetes: What evil bringest thou?

Œdipus: Comest thou the minister of wrath divine?

Philoctetes: Fear nothing.

Œdipus: Do the gods demand my life?

High Priest: If thou givest credit to me, ask me not.

Œdipus: Whatever be the fate which heaven decrees, The safety of my country is concerned, And I will know it.

Philoctetes: Speak.

Œdipus: Have pity on us, Pity the afflicted, pity—

High Priest: Œdipus Deserves more, much more, pity than his people.

Leader of the Chorus.: Œdipus loves them with paternal fondness; To his we join our prayers. O! hear us thou Interpreter of heaven; now hear, and save!

Second Person of the Chorus: We die, O save us! turn aside the wrath Of the angry gods; name the perfidious monster!

Leader of the Chorus.: Name him, and soon the parricide shall die

High Priest: Unhappy men! why will ye press me thus?

Leader of the Chorus.: Speak but the word, he dies, and we are saved.

High Priest: O! ye will tremble but to hear his name, When ye shall know what pangs he must endure. The God, who speaks by me, in pity dooms him To banishment alone; but dreadful ills Await the murderer: driven to fell despair His own rash hand shall to the wrath of heaven Add woes more deep and heavier punishment: Even you shall shudder at his fate, and own Your safety purchased at a rate too dear.

Œdipus: Obey then.

Philoctetes: Speak.

Œdipus: Still obstinate!

High Priest: Remember, If I must speak, that thou didst force me to it.

Œdipus: Insufferable delay! I'll bear no more.

High Priest: Since thou wilt hear it then, 'tis—

Œdipus: Ha! speak, who?

High Priest: 'Tis—Œdipus.

Œdipus: I?

High Priest: Thou, unhappy Prince, Thou art the man.

Second Person of the Chorus: Alas! what do I hear!

Jocaste: Say, can it be, interpreter of heaven? [To Œdipus.] Thou, Œdipus, the murderer of my husband! To whom Jocaste yielded with herself The throne of Thebes: the oracle is false; I know it is; thy virtues must confute it.

Leader of the Chorus.: O! heaven, whose power decrees the fate of mortals, O! name another, or to death devote us!

Philoctetes: [Turning to Œdipus.] Think not I mean to render ill for ill; Or from this strange reverse of fortune take A mean advantage, to return the wrongs I suffered from thy people and from thee: No, Œdipus, I'll do thee noble justice, That justice thou deniest to Philoctetes. Spite of the gods, I think thee innocent, And here I offer thee my willing hand Against thy foes: I cannot hesitate Which I should serve, a pontiff or a king. 'Tis a priest's business, whosoever he be, By whatsoever deity inspired, To pray for, not to curse, his royal master.

Œdipus: Transcendent virtue! execrable traitor! Here I behold a demi-god, and there A base impostor: see the glorious privilege Of altars; thanks to their protecting veil, With lips profane thou hast abused the power Given thee by heaven, to arraign thy king; And yet thou thinkest the sacred ministry Thou hast disgraced shall withhold my wrath: Traitor, thou shouldst have perished at the altar Before those gods whose voice thou hast usurped.

High Priest: My life is in thy hands, and thou art now The master of my fate: seize then the time Whilst yet thou art so, for to-day thy doom Will be pronounced. Tremble, unhappy Prince, Thy reign is past; a hand unseen suspends The fatal sword that glitters o'er thy head: Soon shall thy conscious soul with horror feel The weight of guilt; soon shalt thou quit the throne, Where now thou sittest secure, to wander forth A wretched exile in a distant land; Of wholesome water and of sacred fire Deprived, shalt take thy solitary way, And to the caves and hollow rocks complain. Where'er thou goest, a vengeful God shall still Pursue thy steps; still shalt thou call on death, But call in vain: heaven, that beholds thy fate, Shall hide itself in darkness from thy sight; To guilt and sorrow doomed, thou shall regret Thy life, and wish that thou hadst ne'er been born.

Œdipus: Thus far I have constrained my wrath, and heard thee. Priest, if thy blood were worthy of my sword, Thy life should answer for this insolence: But hence, begone, nor urge my temper further, Thou author of abominable falsehood.

High Priest: Thou callest me hypocrite, and base impostor; Thy father thought not so.

Œdipus: Who? Polybus? My father, saidst thou?

High Priest: Thou wilt know too soon Thy wretched fate: to-day shall give thee birth; To-day shall give thee death: unhappy man, Tell me who gave thee birth, or say with whom Thou livest, beset with sorrows and with crimes For thee alone reserved. O Corinth! Phocis! Detested nuptials! impious wretched race, Too like its parent stem! whose deadly rage Shall fill the world with horror and amaze. Farewell.

SCENE V.

Œdipus, Philoctetes, Jocaste.

Œdipus: His last words fix me to the earth Immovable; my passion is subsided; I know not where I am: methinks some god Descended from above to calm my rage; Who to his priest imparted power divine, And by his sacred voice pronounced my ruin.

Philoctetes: If thou hadst naught to oppose but king to king, I would have fought for Œdipus; but know That Priests are here more formidable foes, Because respected, feared and honored more. Supported by his oracles, the priest Shall often make his sovereign crouch beneath him; Whilst his weak people, dragged in holy chains, Embrace the idol, tread on sacred laws With pious zeal, and think they honor heaven When they betray their master and their king, But above all, when interest, fruitful parent Of riot and licentiousness, increase Their impious rage, and back their insolence.

Œdipus: Alas! thy virtue doubles all my woes, For great as my misfortunes is thy soul; Beneath the weight of care that hangs upon me; Who strives to comfort can but more oppress. What voice is this which from my inmost soul Pours forth complaints? What crime have I committed? Say, vengeful gods, is Œdipus so guilty?

Jocaste: Talk not of guilt, my lord, your dying people Demand a victim; we must save our country; Delay it not: I was the wife of Laius, And I alone should perish: let me seek The wandering spirit of my murdered lord On the infernal shore, and calm his rage: Yes, I will go: may the kind gods accept My life and ask no other sacrifice! May thy Jocaste save her Œdipus!

Œdipus: And wouldest thou die! are there not woes enough Heaped on this head? O cease, my loved Jocaste, This mournful language, I am sunk already Too deep in grief without new miseries, Without thy death to fill my cup of sorrow. Let us go in: I must clear up a doubt Too justly formed, I fear: but follow me.

Jocaste: How couldst thou ever, my lord—

Œdipus: No more: come in, And there confirm my terrors, or remove them.

ACT IV.

SCENE I.

Œdipus, Jocaste.

Œdipus: Jocaste, 'tis in vain: say what thou wilt, These terrible suspicions haunt me still; The priest affrights me; I acquit him now, And even, in secret, am my own accuser. O! I have asked myself some dreadful questions; A thousand strange events, which form my mind Were long effaced, now rush in crowds upon me, And harrow up my soul; the past obstructs, The present but confounds me, and the future Is big with horrid truths; on every side Guilt waits my footsteps.

Jocaste: Will not virtue guard thee? Art thou not sure that thou art innocent?

Œdipus: We're oft more guilty than we think we are.

Jocaste: Disdain the madness of a talking priest, Nor thus excuse him with unmanly fears.

Œdipus: Now in the name of the unhappy king, And angry heaven, let me entreat thee, say, When Laius undertook that fatal journey, Did guards attend him?

Jocaste: I've already told thee, One followed him alone.

Œdipus: And only one?

Jocaste: Superior even to the rank he bore. He was a king, who, like thyself, disdained All irksome pomp, and never would permit An idle train of slaves to march before him. Amidst his happy subjects fearless still, And still unguarded lived in peace and safety, And thought his people's love his best defence.

Œdipus: Thou best of kings, sent by indulgent heaven To mortals here; thou exemplary greatness! Could ever Œdipus his barbarous hand Lift against thee? but if thou canst, Jocaste, Describe him to me.

Jocaste: Since thou wilt recall The sad remembrance, hear what Laius was: Spite of the frost which hoary age had spread O'er his fair temples in declining age, Which yet was vigorous, his eyes sparkled still With all the fire of youth, his wrinkled forehead Beneath, his silver locks attracted awe And reverence from mankind: if I may dare To say it, Laius much resembled thee; With pleasure I behold in Œdipus His virtues and his features thus united. What have I said to alarm thee thus?—

Œdipus: I see Some strange misfortune will o'ertake me soon; The priest, I fear, was by the gods inspired, And but too truly hath foretold my fate: Could I do this, and was it possible?

Jocaste: Are then these holy instruments of heaven Infallible? Their ministry indeed Binds them to the altar, they approach the gods, But they are mortals still; and thinkest thou then Truth is dependent on the flight of birds? Thinkest thou, expiring by the sacred knife, The groaning heifer shall for them alone Remove the veil of dark futurity? Or the gay victims, crowned with flowery garlands, Within their entrails bear the fates of men? O no! to search for truth by ways like these Is to usurp the rights of power supreme; These priests are not what the vile rabble think them, Their knowledge springs from our credulity.

Œdipus: Would it were so! for then I might be happy.

Jocaste: It is: alas! my griefs bear witness to it. Once I was partial to them like thyself, But undeceived at length lament my folly; Heaven hath chastised me for my easy faith In dark mysterious lying oracles, That robbed me of my child; I hate the base Deluders all; had it not been for them, My son had still been living.

Œdipus: Ha! thy son! How didst thou lose him? By what oracles Did the gods speak concerning him?

Jocaste: I'll tell thee What from myself I would have gladly hidden. But 'twas a false one; therefore be not moved. Thou must have heard I had a son by Laius.

A mother's fond disquietude provoked me To ask his fate of the great oracle. Alas! what madness 'tis to wrest from heaven Those secrets which it kindly would conceal: But I was a weak woman, and a mother. Before the priestess' feet I fell submissive, And thus her answer was; for O, too well I must remember what but to repeat Now makes me tremble; but thou wilt forgive me: "Thy son shall slay his father, sacrilegious, Incestuous parricide." Shall I go on?

Œdipus: Well, very well—

Jocaste: In short, it then foretold me, This son, this monster should pollute my bed; That I, his mother, should embrace my son, Just recent from the murder of his father. That thus united by these dreadful ties, I should bear children to this hapless child. You seem to be disordered at my story, And dread perhaps to hear the sad remainder.

Œdipus: Proceed: what did you with the wretched infant. Object of wrath divine?

Jocaste: Believed the gods; Piously cruel, sacrificed my child, And stifled all a mother's tenderness: In vain the clamors of parental love Condemned the rigid laws of partial heaven: Alas! I meant to save the tender victim From his hard fate that threatened future guilt, And doomed him to involuntary crimes: I thought to triumph o'er the oracle, And in compassion gave him up to death. Cruel compassion, and destructive too! Deceitful darkness of a false prediction! What did I reap from my inhuman care, Did it prolong my wretched husband's life? Alas! cut off in full prosperity, He fell by the unknown hands of base assassins, Not by his son. Thus were they both torn from me: I lost my child, and could not save his father. By my example taught, avoid my errors, Banish these idle fears, and calm thy soul.

Œdipus: After the dreadful secret thou hast told me, It were not fit I should conceal my own: Hear then my tale; perchance when thou shalt know The sad relation, which they bear each other, Thou too wilt tremble: Born the natural heir To Corinth's throne, from Corinth far removed, I look with horror on my native land: One day—that fatal day I well remember, For O! 'tis ever present to my thoughts, And dreadful to my soul—my youthful hands, For the first time their solemn gift prepared An offering to the gods, when lo! the gates Throughout the temple on a sudden stood Self-opened, and the pillars streamed with blood; The altars shook; a hand invisible Threw back my offerings, and in thunder thus A horrid voice addressed me: "Come not here, Stain not the holy threshold with thy feet, The gods have from the living cut thee off Indignant, nor will e'er accept thy gifts; Go, take thy offerings to the furies, seek The serpents that stand ready to devour thee; These are thy gods, begone, and worship them." While terror seized me at these dreadful words, Again the voice alarmed me, and foretold All those sad crimes which heaven to thee denounced Against thy son; said, I should slay my father, O gods! and be the husband of my mother.

Jocaste: Where am I? what malicious dæmon joined Our hands, to make us thus supremely wretched?

Œdipus: Reserve thy tears for something still more dreadful; Now list and tremble: fearful of myself, Lest I should e'er fulfil the dire prediction, Or oppose heaven, I left my native land, Broke from the arms of a distracted mother, Wandered from place to place, disguised my birth, My family, and name, by one kind friend Attended; yet, in my disastrous journey, The God who guided my sad footsteps oft Strengthened my arm, and crowned me with success: But happier had it been for Œdipus, If he had fallen with glory in the field, And by his death prevented all his woes: I was reserved to be a parricide: The hand of heaven, so long suspended o'er me, Hath from my eyes at length removed the veil Of Ignorance, and now I see it all: I do remember, in the fields of Phocis (Nor know I how I could so long forget The great event) that in a narrow way I met two warriors in a splendid car: The path was strait, and we disputed it: An idle contest for us both; but I Was young and haughty, from my earliest years Bred up to pride that flowed in with my blood; An unknown stranger in a foreign land, I thought myself upon my father's throne, And whomso'er I chanced to meet, esteemed As my own vassals, born but to obey me: I rushed upon them, and with furious arm Their rapid coursers stopped in full career; Hurled from their chariot the intrepid pair. Forward advanced in rage, and both attacked me: The combat was not long, for victory soon Declared for Œdipus. Immortal powers! Whether from hatred or from love I know not, But surely on that day ye fought for me. I saw them both expiring at my feet, And one of them, I do remember well, Who seemed in age well-stricken, as he lay Gasping on the earth, looked earnestly upon me, Held out his arms, and would have spoke: I saw The tears flow plenteous from his half-closed eyes: Methought when I did wound him my shocked soul, All conqueror as I was—you shake, Jocaste.

Jocaste: My lord, see Phorbas comes; this way they lead him.

Œdipus: 'Tis well: my doubts will then be satisfied.

SCENE II.

Œdipus, Jocaste, Phorbas, Attendants.

Œdipus: Come hither, thou unfortunate old man; The sight of him alarms my conscious soul; Confused remembrance tortures me; I dread To look on, or to question him.

Phorbas: O queen, Is this the day appointed for my death; Hast thou decreed it? Never but to me Wert thou unjust.

Jocaste: Fear not, but hear the king, And answer him.

Phorbas: The king?

Jocaste: Thou standest before him.

Phorbas: Ye gods! is this the successor of Laius?

Œdipus: Waste not the time thus idly, but inform me, Thou wert the only witness of his death, And wounded, so 'tis said, in his defence.

Phorbas: He's dead, and let his ashes rest in peace; Embitter not my fate, nor thus insult A faithful subject wounded by thy hand.

Œdipus: I wound thee? I?

Phorbas: Now satiate thy revenge, And put an end to this unhappy life; The poor remains of blood which then escaped thee Now thou mayest shed; and since thou must remember The fatal place where Laius—

Œdipus: Spare the rest: It is enough: I see it now: 'twas I: Ye gods! my eyes are opened.

Jocaste: Can it be?

Œdipus: And art thou he whom my unhappy rage Attacked at Daulis in the narrow path? O yes it is, must be so: in vain myself Would I deceive, all speaks too plain against me, I know thee but too well.

Phorbas: I saw him fall, My royal master fall beneath thy hand: Thou didst the crime, and I have suffered for it: A prison was my fate, and thine a throne.

Œdipus: Away: I soon shall do thee ample justice, Thee and myself; leave then to me the care Of my own punishment: begone, and save me At least the painful sight of innocence, Which I have made unhappy.

SCENE III.

Œdipus, Jocaste.

Œdipus: O Jocaste! For cruel fate forbids me ever more To call thee by the tender name of wife; Thou seest my crimes; no longer bound to love; Strike now, and free thyself from the dread thought Of being mine.

Jocaste: Alas!

Œdipus: Take, take this sword, The instrument of my unhappy rage; Receive, and use it for a noble purpose, And plunge it in my breast.

Jocaste: What wouldst thou do! O stop thy furious grief, be calm, and live.

Œdipus: Canst thou have pity on a wretch like me? No, I must die.

Jocaste: Thou must not: hear Jocaste, O hear her prayers!

Œdipus: I will not, must not hear thee. I slew thy husband.

Jocaste: And thou gavest me one.

Œdipus: I did, but 'twas by guilt.

Jocaste: Involuntary.

Œdipus: No matter, still 'twas guilt.

Jocaste: O height of woe!

Œdipus: O fatal nuptials! once such envied bliss!

Jocaste: Such be it still, for still thou art my husband.

Œdipus: O no! I am not; this destructive hand Hath broke the sacred tie, and deep involved Thy kingdom in my ruin. O! avoid me, Fear the vindictive God who still pursues The wretched Œdipus; I fear myself, My timid virtue serves but to confound me; Perhaps my fate may reach even thee, Jocaste; Pity thyself, pity the hapless victims That perish daily for my guilt; O strike, And save thy Œdipus from future crimes.

Jocaste: Do not accuse, do not condemn thyself; Thou art unhappy, but thou art not guilty: Thou didst not know whose blood thy hand had shed In Daulis' fatal conflict; when remembrance Calls forth the melancholy deed, I must Weep for myself, but should not punish thee. Live therefore—

Œdipus: No; it is impossible: Farewell, Jocaste! whither must I go, O whither must I drag this hateful being? What clime accursed, or what disastrous shore Shall hide my crimes, and bury my despair? Still must I wander on from clime to clime, Or rise by murder to another throne? Shall I to Corinth bend my way, where fate Hath heavier crimes in store for Œdipus? O Corinth! ne'er on thy detested borders—

SCENE IV.

Œdipus, Jocaste, Dimas.

Dimas: My lord, this moment is arrived a stranger, He says, from Corinth, and desires admittance.

Œdipus: I'll go and meet him—fare thee well, Jocaste: But stop thy tears; no more shalt thou behold The wretched Œdipus; it is determined: My reign is past; thou hast no husband now, I am no more a sovereign, nor Jocaste's. Oppressed with ills I go, in search of climes, Where far removed from thee and from my country, I still may act as shall become a king, Worthy of thee, and justify the tears Thou sheddest for Œdipus: farewell! forever.

ACT V.

SCENE I.

Œdipus, Araspes, Dimas, Attendants.

Œdipus: Weep not for me, my friends, nor thus regret Your sovereign's fate: I wish for banishment; To me 'tis pleasure; for I know 'twill make My people happy: you must lose your king, But shall preserve his country. When I first Came to the throne of Thebes, I served it well; And, as I mounted, now I shall descend In glory: honor shall attend my fall: I leave my country, kingdom, children, all. Then hear me now, hear my last parting words; A king you must have; let him be my choice; Take Philoctetes: he is generous, noble, Virtuous, and brave; his father was a king, And he the friend of Hercules; let him Succeed me: I must hence.—Go, search out Phorbas; Bid him not fear, but come this moment hither, I must bequeath him something; he deserves it: I'll take my farewell as a monarch ought. Go, bring the stranger to me—stay ye here.

SCENE II.

Œdipus, Araspes, Icarus, Attendants.

Œdipus: Ha! is it thou, my much-loved Icarus! The faithful guardian of my infant years, Favorite and friend of Polybus, my father, What brought thee hither?

Icarus: Polybus is dead.

Œdipus: Alas? my father!

Icarus: 'Twas what we expected; For he had filled the measure of his days, And died in good old age; these eyes beheld it. Where are ye now, mistaken oracles! That shook my timid virtue, and foretold That I should prove a guilty parricide? My father's dead, ye meant but to deceive me; These hands are not polluted with his blood: The slave of error, I have wandered long In darkness, busied in a fruitless toil, And to remove imaginary ills, Have made my life a scene of real woes, The offspring of my fond credulity. How deep must be the color of my fate When miseries like this can bring relief! Bliss spring from sorrow, and a father's death Shall be accepted as the gift of heaven! But I must hence, and to his ashes pay The tribute due:—ha! silent, and in tears!

Icarus: Ought I to speak? O heaven!

Œdipus: Hast thou aught more Of ill to tell me?

Icarus: For a moment grant me Your private ear.

Œdipus: Retire.—[To the attendants.] What can this mean?

Icarus: Think not of Corinth: thither, if thou goest, Thy death is certain.

Œdipus: Who shall banish me From my own kingdom?

Icarus: To the throne of Corinth Another heir succeeds.

Œdipus: Ye gods! is this The last sad stroke which I am born to suffer, Or will ye still pursue me? Fate, go on And persecute, thou shalt not conquer me: Let us away to my rebellious subjects, I'll go to be their scourge, if not their king, And find at least an honorable death. But say, what stranger has usurped my throne?

Icarus: He is the son-in-law of Polybus, Who on his head did place the diadem In his last moments; the obedient people Hail their new sovereign.

Œdipus: Has my father too Betrayed me, sided with my faithless subjects, And drove me from my throne?

Icarus: He did but justice, For thou wert not his son.

Œdipus: Ha! Icarus!

Icarus: With terror and regret I must reveal The dreadful secret, Corinth—

Œdipus: Not his son!

Icarus: Thou art not. Polybus, oppressed by conscience, Dying declared it; to the royal blood Of Corinth's kings he yielded up his throne: I who alone enjoyed his confidence, And therefore dreaded the new sovereign's power, Fled to implore thy aid.

Œdipus: Who am I then, If not the son of Polybus?

Icarus: The gods, Who trusted to my hands thy infant years, In shades of darkest night conceal thy birth; I only know, that soon as born condemned To death, and on a desert hill exposed, Thou but for me hadst perished.

Œdipus: Thus with life Began my sorrows, a detested object Even from my cradle, and accursed by all. Where didst thou light on me?

Icarus: On mount Citheron,

Œdipus: Near Thebes?

Icarus: In that deserted place, a Theban, Who called himself thy father, left thee; there To perish: some kind God conducted me That way; I pitied, took thee in my arms, Revived, and cherished thee: to Corinth then Carried my little charge, and to the king Presented thee; who, mark thy wondrous fate! His child just dead, adopted thee his son, And by that stroke of policy confirmed His tottering power: As son of Polybus Thou wert brought up by him who had preserved thee: The throne of Corinth never was thy right, But conscience robbed thee of what chance bestowed.

Œdipus: Immortal powers, who rule the fate of kings! Am I thus doomed in one unhappy day To suffer such variety of woe! On a frail mortal shall your miracles Be thus exhausted! But inform me, friend, This old man, from whose hands you took me, say, Hast thou beheld him since that fatal hour?

Icarus: Never: perhaps he's dead, he who alone Could tell thee the strange secret of thy birth; But on my mind his image is engraved So deeply, I should know him well.

Œdipus: Alas! Wretch that I am! why should I wish to find him? Rather, submissive to the will of heaven Should I keep close the veil that o'er my eyes

Spreads its benignant shade: too well already I see my fate; more knowledge would but show New horrors; and yet, spite of all my woes, Urged on by fatal curiosity, I thirst for more: I cannot bear to rest In sad suspense: to doubt is to be wretched: I dread the torch that lights me to my ruin: I fear to know myself, yet cannot long Remain unknown.

SCENE III.

Œdipus, Icarus, Phorbas.

Œdipus: Ha! Phorbas! come this way.

Icarus: Surprising! sure the more I look, the more— 'Tis he, my lord, it must be he.

Phorbas: Forgive me [To Icarus] If still that face unknown—

Icarus: Dost thou remember? On mount Citheron—

Phorbas: How!

Icarus: The child you gave me, The child to death—

Phorbas: What dost thou say? remember, Remember what?

Icarus: Thou hast no cause to fear; Le not alarmed: thou mayest rejoice, that infant Was—Œdipus.

Phorbas: The lightning blast thee, wretch! What hast thou said?

Icarus: Doubt not, my lord, whatever [To Œdipus.] This Theban says, he gave thee to my arms; Thy fate is known; this old man is thy father.

Œdipus: What complicated misery! Alas! [To Phorbas.] If thou art indeed my father, will the gods Ever suffer me to shed thy blood?

Phorbas: O no! For thou art not my son.

Œdipus: And didst not thou Expose me in my infancy?

Phorbas: My lord, Permit me to retire, and hide from thee The dreadful truth.

Œdipus: No, Phorbas; by the gods I beg thee, tell me all.

Phorbas: Begone, avoid Thy children, and thy queen.

Œdipus: Now answer me, For to resist is vain: that infant, doomed To death by thee, say, didst thou give it him? [Pointing to **Icarus: Phorbas**: I did: and would that day had been my last!]

Œdipus: And of what country was that child?

Phorbas: Of Thebes.

Œdipus: And thou art not his father?

Phorbas: No: alas! Sprung from a nobler, but more wretched race—

Œdipus: Who was he then?

Phorbas: My lord, what would you do? [Throwing himself at the feet of Œdipus.]

Œdipus: Speak, speak, I say.

Phorbas: Jocaste was his mother.

Icarus: [Looking at Œdipus.] Behold the fruit of all my generous care!

Phorbas: What have we done?

Œdipus: I thought it must be so.

Icarus: My lord—

Œdipus: Away, begone, this moment leave me: The dreadful gifts ye have bestowed on me Must have their recompense; and ye have cause To fear my wrath, for ye preserved my life.

SCENE IV.

Œdipus: At length the dire prediction is fulfilled, And Œdipus is now, though innocent, A base, incestuous parricide: O virtue! Thou fatal empty name; thou who didst guide My hapless days, thou hadst not power to stop The current of my fate: alas! I fell Into the snare by trying to avoid it: Heaven led me on to guilt, and sunk a pit Beneath my sliding feet: I was the slave Of some unknown, some unrelenting power, That used me for its instrument of vengeance: These are my crimes, remorseless cruel gods! Yours was the guilt, and ye have punished me. Where am I? what dark shade thus from my eyes Covers the light of heaven? the walls are stained With blood; the furies shake their torches at me; The lightnings flash; hell opens her wide gates: O Laius! O my father! art thou there? I see the deadly wound these hands had made; Revenge thee now on this abhorred monster, A monster who defiled the bed of her Who bore him: lead me to the dark abode, That I may strike fresh terror to the hearts Of guilty beings by my punishment: Lead on, I'll follow thee.

SCENE V.

Œdipus, Jocaste, Ægina, Chorus.

Jocaste: O Œdipus, Dispel my fears, thy dreadful cries alarm me.

Œdipus: Open, thou earth, and swallow me!

Jocaste: Alas! What sad misfortune moves thee thus?

Œdipus: My crimes.

Jocaste: My lord!—

lf0060-08_figure_005 Œdipus: Away, Jocaste.

Jocaste: Cruel husband!

Œdipus: O stop! what name is that? am I thy husband? Do not say husband: we shall hate each other.

Jocaste: What sayest thou?

Œdipus: 'Tis enough: I have fulfilled My horrid fate: know, Laius was my father; I am thy son.

Leader of the Chorus.: O guilt!

Second Person of the Chorus: O dreadful day!

Jocaste: Ægina, drag me from this horrid place!

Ægina: Alas!

Jocaste: If thou hast pity on Jocaste, If without horror thou canst now approach me, Assist me now, compassionate thy queen!

Leader of the Chorus.: Ye gods! and is it thus your vengeance ceases? Take back your cruel gifts, 'twere better far That we had suffered still.

SCENE VI.

Jocaste, Ægina, High Priest, Chorus.

High Priest: Attend, ye people, And know, a milder sun now beams upon you: At length the baleful pestilence is fled, The graves once more are closed, and death hath left us; The God of heaven and earth declares his goodness In peals of thunder: hark! [Thunder and lightning.]

Jocaste: What dreadful flashes! Where am I? heaven! what do I hear! Barbarians—

High Priest: 'Tis done: the gods are satisfied: no more Doth Laius from the tomb cry out for vengeance: Jocaste, thou mayest live and reign; the blood Of Œdipus sufficeth.

Chorus: Gracious heaven!

Jocaste: My son! and must I call him husband too! Dear dreadful names! is he then dead?

High Priest: He lives, But from the living and the dead cut off, Deprived of light: I saw him plunge this sword, Stained with his father's blood, into his eyes: This fatal moment has to Thebes restored Her safety: such are the decrees of heaven: Which, as it wills, decides the fate of mortals, All-powerful to save or to destroy. Its wrath is all exhausted on thy son, And thou art pardoned.

Jocaste: Punish then thyself. [Stabs herself.] Jocaste, thus reserved for horrid incest, Death is the only good remaining for me: Laius, receive my blood: I follow thee: I have lived virtuous, and shall die with pleasure.

Chorus: Unhappy queen, and sad calamity!

Jocaste: Weep only for my son, who still survives. Priests, and you Thebans, who were once my subjects, Honor my ashes, and remember ever, That midst the horrors which oppressed me, still I could reproach the gods; for heaven alone Was guilty of the crime, and not Jocaste.

End

www.ingramcontent.com/pod-product-compliance
Lightning Source LLC
Chambersburg PA
CBHW030523100426
42813CB00001B/128